Disabilities and Differences

We All Play

Rebecca Rissman

Heinemann Library
Chicago, Illinois

an imprint of Capstone Global Library LLC
Chicago, Illinois

Customer Service 888-454-2279
Visit our website at www.heinemannraintree.com

Printed in the United States of America in Eau Claire, Wisconsin. 010615 008684RP

15 14 13
10 9 8 7 6 5 4 3

Library of Congress Cataloging-in-Publication Data
Rissman, Rebecca.
We all play / Rebecca Rissman.
p. cm. -- (Disabilities and differences)
Includes bibliographical references and index.
ISBN 978-1-4329-2151-4 (hc) -- ISBN 978-1-4329-2157-6 (pb)
1. Play--Juvenile literature. 2. Child development. I. Title.
LB1139.35.P55R57 2008
306.4'81--dc22
2008029749

Acknowledgments
The author and publisher are grateful to the following for permission to reproduce photographs: ©agefotostock p. 4 (John Birdsall); ©Corbis pp. 7 (zefa/Mika), 14 (Reuters/Claro Cortes IV); ©drr.net pp. 12 (Leah Warkentin), 15 (Janine Wiedel), 18 (Leah Warkentin); ©Getty Images pp. 6 (Tara Moore), 8 (Brent Stirton), 9 (Siri Stafford), 10 (Robert Prezioso), 11 (Gary Buss), 12 (NBAE/D. Clarke Evans), 19 (Michael Cogliantry), 20 (Realistic Reflections), 21 (Celia Peterson), 23 top (Realistic Reflections), 23 middle (Brent Stirton), 23 bottom (Robert Prezioso/Getty Images); ©Shutterstock pp. 13 (Koer), 16 (Damir Karan), 17 (Loesevsky Pavel), 22 (M W Productions).

Cover image used with permission of ©Corbis (Andy Aitchison). Back cover image used with permission of ©Getty Images (Siri Stafford).

Contents

Differences

We are all different.

Playing

We play to learn.

We play to laugh.

We play to explore.

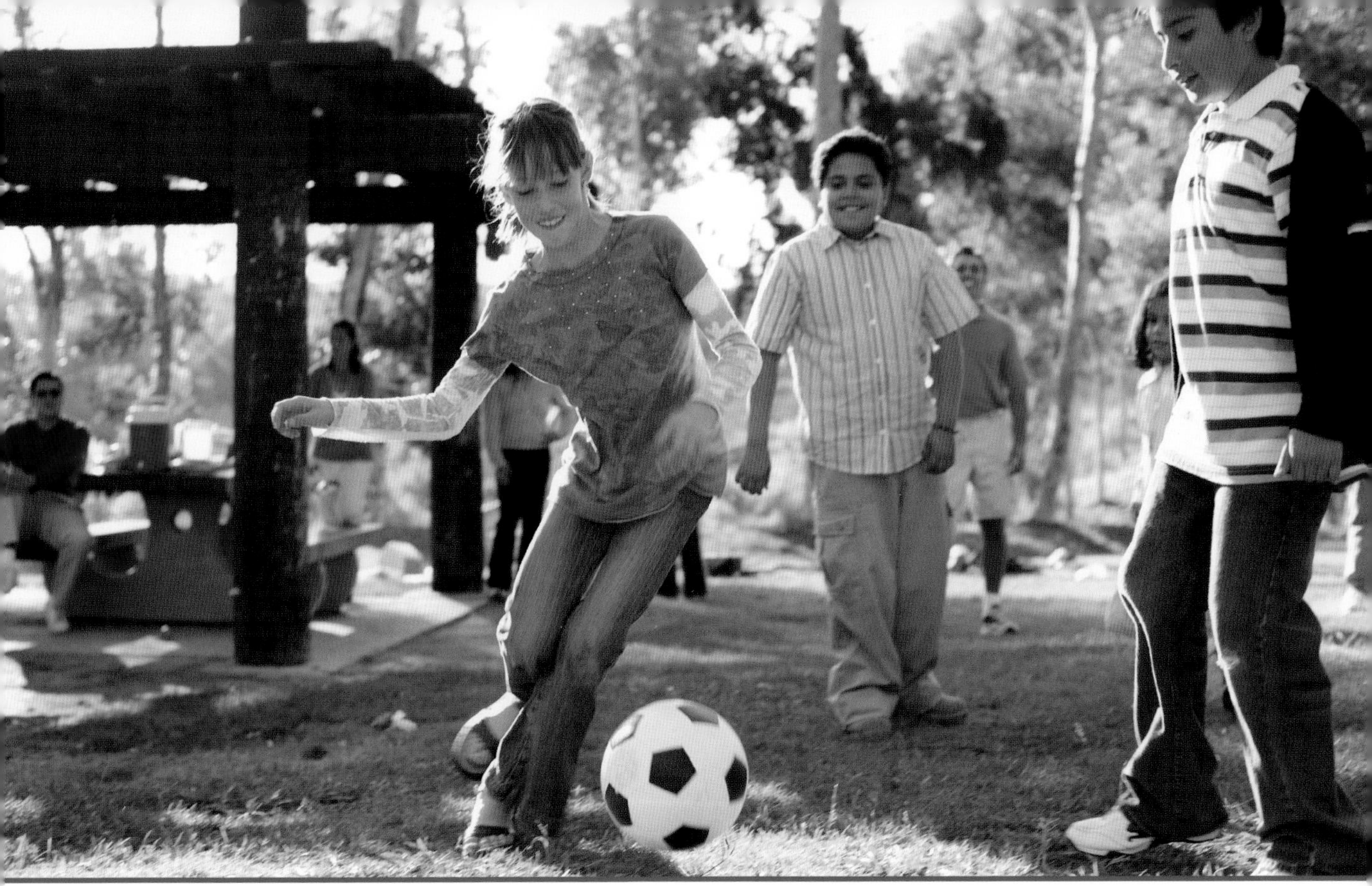

We play to exercise.

How We Play

We play in different ways.

We play in different places.

CAMARILLO
35
SPURS
42
SPURS
42

Some people play together.

Some people play alone.

超
越
红双喜
DHS
FANG

Some people play games.

Some people play music.

Some people play video games.

Some people play with toys.

Some people play outside.

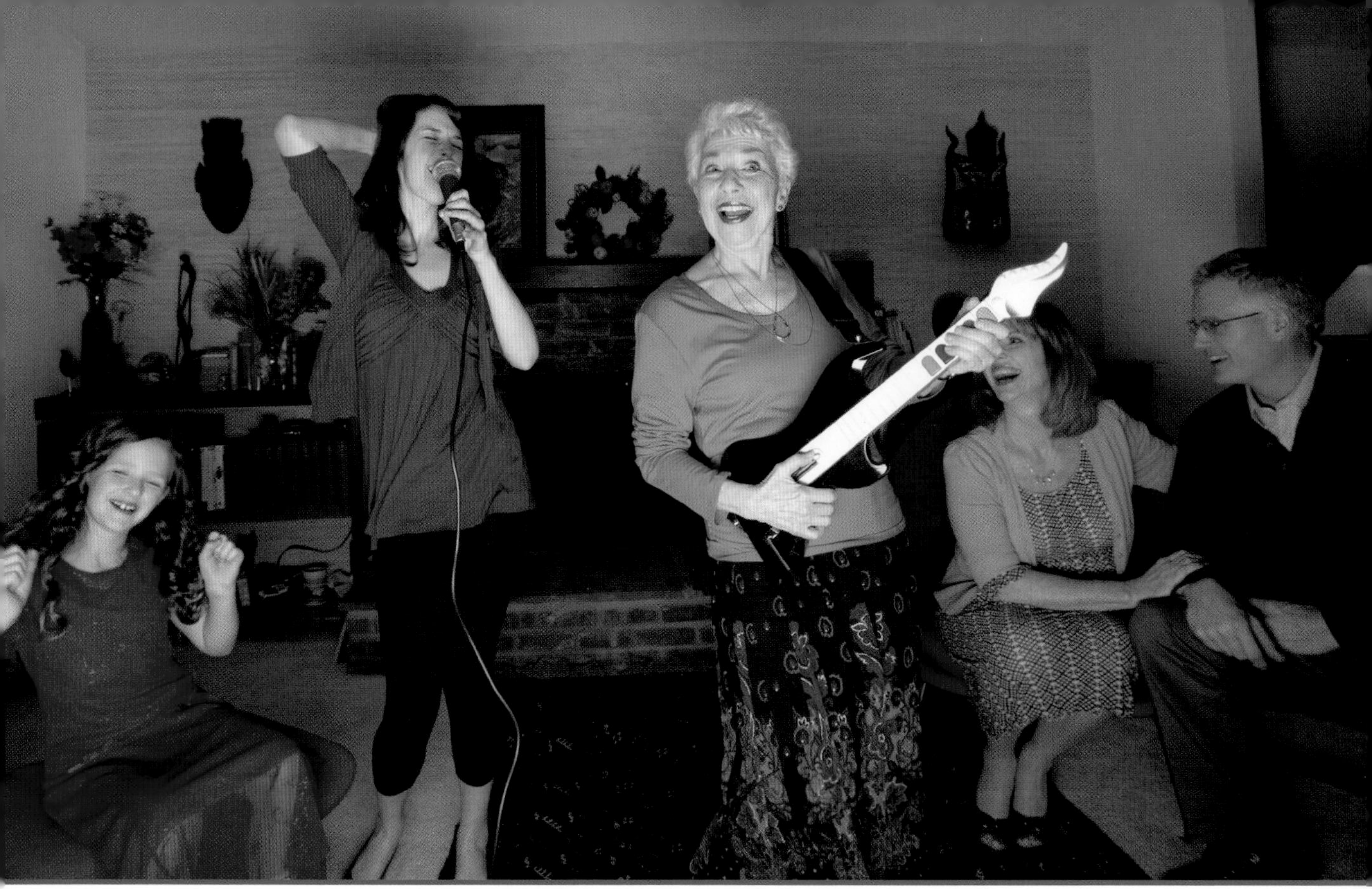

Some people play inside.

Some people play at school.

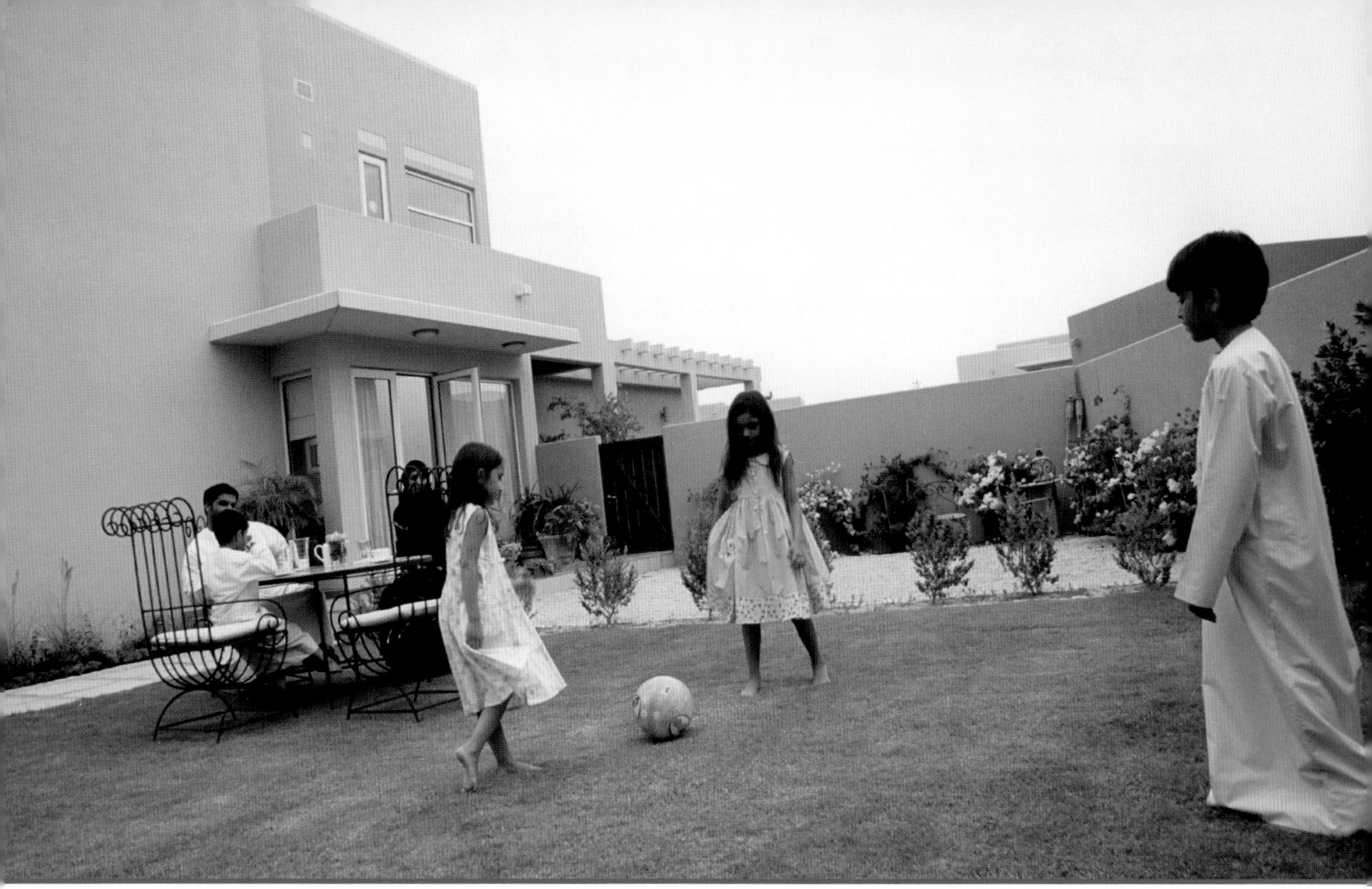

Some people play at home.

We Are All Different

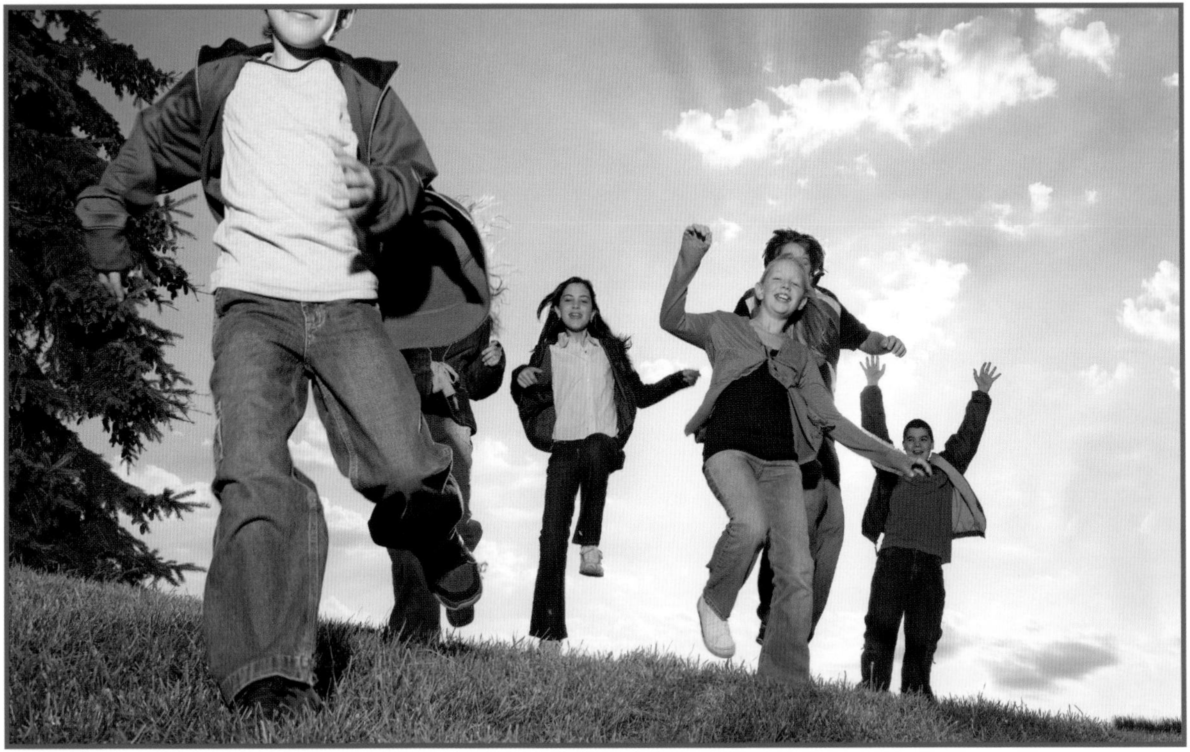

We are all different.

How do you play?

Words to Know

brace something worn to help people grow and move in healthy ways

crutches long poles that people use to walk

wheelchair a chair with wheels. Some people use wheelchairs to get around.

This section includes related vocabulary words that can help students learn about this topic. Use these words to explore play.

Index

Note to Parents and Teachers

Before reading

Ask children to form pairs. Ask them to talk to a partner about their favorite game. Then ask each partner to tell you what their partner likes to play. Collect the answers and list them under sports, board games, music, computer games, and playground games on the board.

After reading

Tell the children to look through magazines and catalogues and to cut out pictures of people playing sports, music, or games. Make a collage of these pictures and help the children to write labels for each activity. Then lead children in a discussion about the many ways that people can play.